ITS A BUGS WORLD SCARY AND SPOOKY BUGS

BABY PROFESSOR
EDUCATION KIDS

Bugs are creepy. Bugs can
often be seen as an annoyance
to humans, but they play
a huge part in our world.

The golden silk orb-weavers are also banana spiders. Golden Orb Weavers are known to occasionally eat prey as big as small birds and even snakes.

Rhinoceros Beetle is one of the strongest animals in the world. The rhino beetle can lift 850 times its body weight.

The Bullet Ant stretches almost 1.5 inches in length. Bullet ants are appropriately named since the aid of a sting from just one of them is compared to being shot with a bullet.

Africanized honey bees are also called killer bees. Africanized honey bees are the result of breeding bees from southern Africa with local Brazilian honey bees. Africanized honey bees travel greater distances to attack.

Spiny Leaf insect is a large species of stick insect endemic to Australia. Spiny Leaf Insects are phasmids, which means they are insects that both eat and resemble leaves and sticks.

The goliath bird-
eating spider is the
world's heaviest
spider. Goliath Bird-
eaters can grow up
to a foot long with
one inch long fangs.

Saddleback caterpillar is the larva of a species of moth native to eastern North America. It has a pair of fleshy horns at either end. These and most of the rest of the body bear urticating hairs that secrete an irritating venom.

9 798869 450234